GRAPHIC DINOSAURS

HADROSAURUS

THE DUCK-BILLED DINOSAUR

ILLUSTRATED BY TERRY RILEY

PowerKiDS
press.

New York

Published in 2010 by The Rosen Publishing Group, Inc.
29 East 21st Street, New York, NY 10010

Designed and produced by
David West Books

Designed and written by Rob Shone
Editor: Ronne Randall
U.S. Editor: Kara Murray
Consultant: Steve Parker, Senior Scientific Fellow, Zoological Society of London
Photographic credits: 5t, Ballista; 5m, Benh LIEU SONG; 5bl, Rainer Ebert; 30l–30m, The Academy of Natural Sciences; 30r, ideonexus.

Library of Congress Cataloging-in-Publication Data

Shone, Rob.
Hadrosaurus : the duck-billed dinosaur / Rob Shone ; illustrated by Terry Riley.
p. cm. — (Graphic dinosaurs)
Includes index.
ISBN 978-1-4358-8591-2 (lib. bdg.) — ISBN 978-1-4358-8598-1 (pbk.)
ISBN 978-1-4358-8599-8 (6-pack)
1. Hadrosauridae—Juvenile literature. I. Riley, Terry, ill. II. Title.
QE862.O65S46 2009
567.914—dc22
                                        2009016048

Manufactured in China

CONTENTS

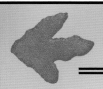

WHAT IS A HADROSAURUS?

HADROSAURUS MEANS "STURDY LIZARD"

Hadrosaurus used its stiff tail to stay balanced when it ran.

Hadrosaurus had hundreds of teeth at the back of its mouth. New teeth grew throughout the Hadrosaurus's life to replace old and worn ones.

Instead of front teeth, Hadrosaurus had a horny beak at the end of its snout.

Hadrosaurus's back legs were powerful and much longer than its front ones.

The soles of Hadrosaurus's back feet were covered with soft pads that acted as cushions.

Hadrosaurus had hooves, rather than claws, on its three toes.

HADROSAURUS WAS A DINOSAUR THAT LIVED AROUND 84 MILLION TO 71 MILLION YEARS AGO, DURING THE **CRETACEOUS PERIOD**. **FOSSILS** OF ITS SKELETON HAVE BEEN FOUND IN NORTH AMERICA.

An adult Hadrosaurus measured up to 30 feet (9 m) long and 10 feet (3 m) high and weighed 7.5 tons (6,803 kg).

The skull of an Edmontosaurus (a close relative of Hadrosaurus) ended in a horny beak. This shows why they are called duck-billed dinosaurs.

TEETH

Although it had no teeth at the front of its mouth, it had hundreds of rough, broad teeth at the back, arranged in rows in its top and bottom jaws. Their two sets of teeth came together at an angle, grinding mouthfuls of food into small pieces ready to be swallowed and easily digested.

DUCK BILLS

Hadrosaurus is known as a duck-billed dinosaur. Like all the dinosaurs in its family, Hadrosaurus had a broad beak similar to a present-day duck's. Hadrosaurus used it to bite through tough ferns and flowering plants.

ON THE RUN

Hadrosaurus herds spent their days walking on all four legs, feeding on ferns and juicy leaves. If they needed to, they could raise themselves up onto their powerful back legs to outrun enemies, such as *Tyrannosaurus rex*.

Hadrosauruses were plant eaters that lived in herds, as are present-day cattle (top). Like zebra and wildebeest (right), they could run quickly to escape from danger.

PART ONE... DANGEROUS DAYS

THE HADROSAURUSES BELLOW OUT A WARNING CRY. THEY HAVE SPOTTED A DEINOSUCHUS HIDING IN THE RIVERBED. THE HUGE CROCODILE COULD EASILY GRAB AN ADULT HADROSAURUS FROM THE RIVERBANK, AND THE HERD IS EAGER TO SEE IT GONE.

THE DEINOSUCHUS USES SURPRISE TO CATCH ITS PREY. THERE IS NO REASON FOR IT TO STAY NOW THAT THE HADROSAURUSES HAVE SEEN IT, SO IT LAZILY SWIMS AWAY.

THE HADROSAURUSES ARE MORE WATCHFUL THAN USUAL BECAUSE THEIR NESTS ARE NOT FAR FROM THE RIVER.

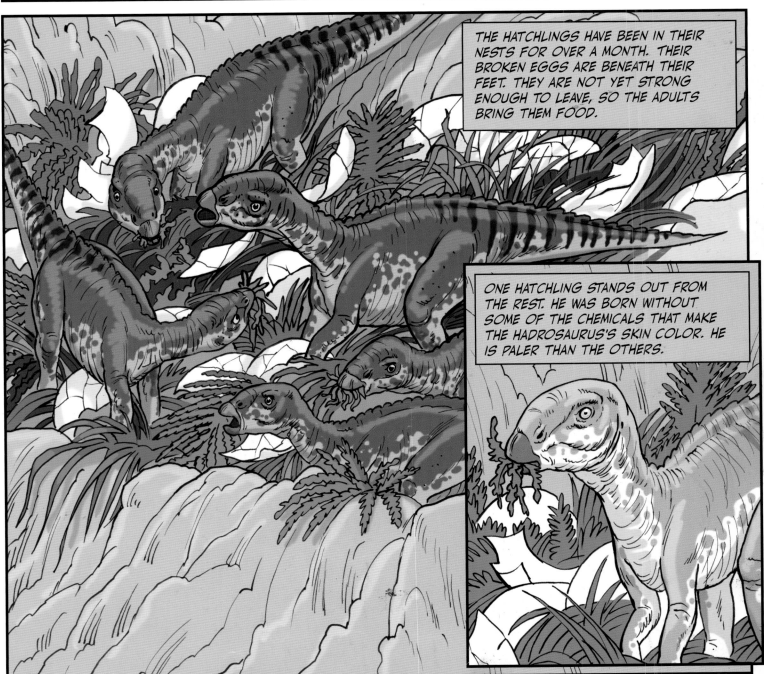

THE HATCHLINGS HAVE BEEN IN THEIR NESTS FOR OVER A MONTH. THEIR BROKEN EGGS ARE BENEATH THEIR FEET. THEY ARE NOT YET STRONG ENOUGH TO LEAVE, SO THE ADULTS BRING THEM FOOD.

ONE HATCHLING STANDS OUT FROM THE REST. HE WAS BORN WITHOUT SOME OF THE CHEMICALS THAT MAKE THE HADROSAURUS'S SKIN COLOR. HE IS PALER THAN THE OTHERS.

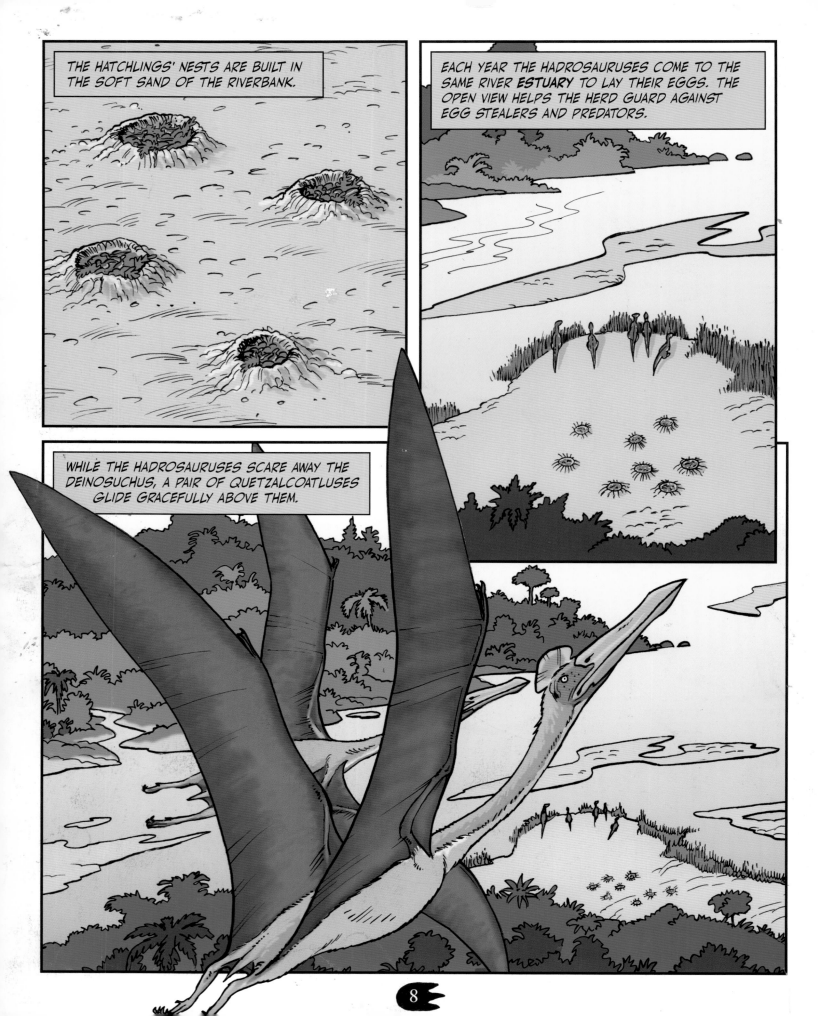

THE HATCHLINGS' NESTS ARE BUILT IN THE SOFT SAND OF THE RIVERBANK.

EACH YEAR THE HADROSAURUSES COME TO THE SAME RIVER **ESTUARY** TO LAY THEIR EGGS. THE OPEN VIEW HELPS THE HERD GUARD AGAINST EGG STEALERS AND PREDATORS.

WHILE THE HADROSAURUSES SCARE AWAY THE DEINOSUCHUS, A PAIR OF QUETZALCOATLUSES GLIDE GRACEFULLY ABOVE THEM.

THEY HAVE NOTICED THAT THE NESTS ARE UNGUARDED. BELOW THEM THE HATCHLINGS ARE UNAWARE OF THE LARGE FLYING REPTILES AS THEY TURN...

...AND SWOOP DOWN TO THE GROUND.

RARRKK!

RARRKK!

A HUNGRY QUETZALCOATLUS LIKES TO EAT CARRION. IT WILL ALSO EAT ANY LIZARD OR SMALL DINOSAUR IT CAN CATCH AS IT WALKS ALONG THE GROUND. THOSE NESTS FILLED WITH HATCHLINGS WILL PROVIDE IT WITH LOTS OF TASTY TREATS.

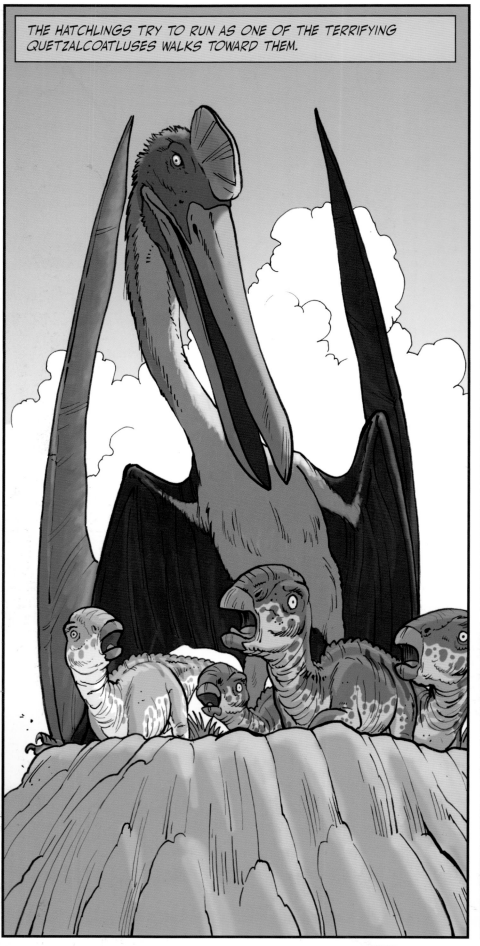

THE HATCHLINGS TRY TO RUN AS ONE OF THE TERRIFYING QUETZALCOATLUSES WALKS TOWARD THEM.

THE REPTILE BENDS OVER THE PALE HATCHLING, WHO SCREAMS LOUDLY.

YAAARRRK!!!

AN ADULT HEARS THE HATCHLING.

RUSHING FROM THE RIVER, THE ADULTS CHARGE AT THE QUETZALCOATLUSES. THE REPTILES ARE NO MATCH FOR THE ANGRY HADROSAURUSES.

SSCHHAR!

BROUARR!

RARRKK!

THEY STAGGER AND STUMBLE ACROSS THE SAND...

...AND LAUNCH THEMSELVES INTO THE AIR.

THE PALE HATCHLING WATCHES THE QUETZALCOATLUSES FLY AWAY. HE HAS HAD A NARROW ESCAPE AND WILL PROBABLY HAVE MORE BEFORE HE IS FULLY GROWN.

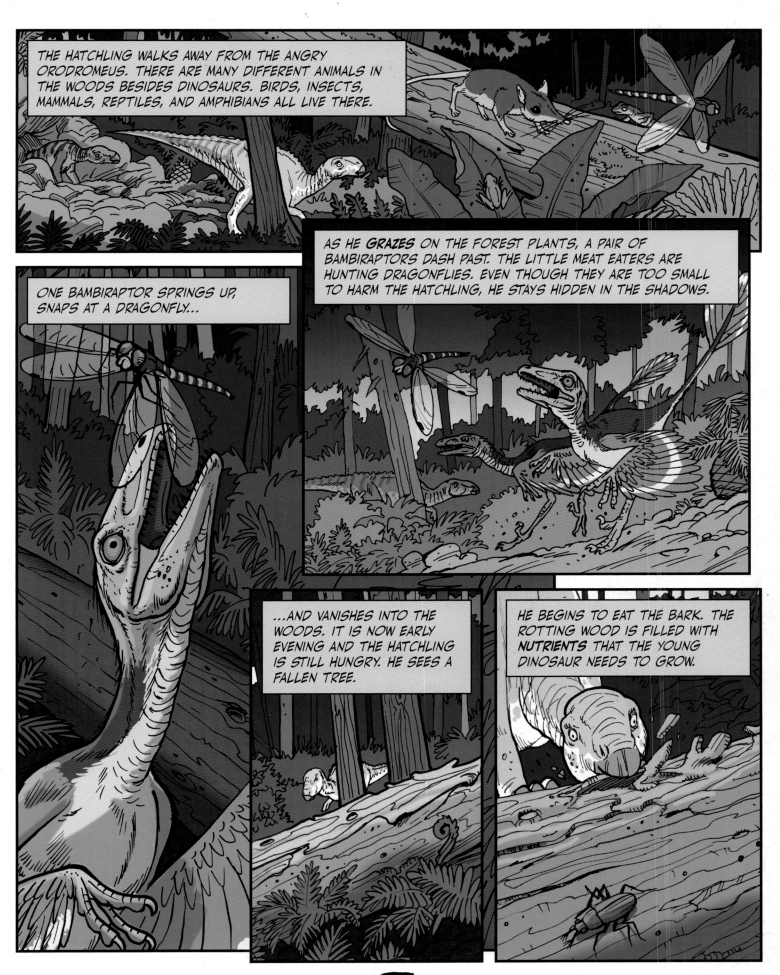

THE HATCHLING WALKS AWAY FROM THE ANGRY ORODROMEUS. THERE ARE MANY DIFFERENT ANIMALS IN THE WOODS BESIDES DINOSAURS. BIRDS, INSECTS, MAMMALS, REPTILES, AND AMPHIBIANS ALL LIVE THERE.

ONE BAMBIRAPTOR SPRINGS UP, SNAPS AT A DRAGONFLY...

AS HE **GRAZES** ON THE FOREST PLANTS, A PAIR OF BAMBIRAPTORS DASH PAST. THE LITTLE MEAT EATERS ARE HUNTING DRAGONFLIES. EVEN THOUGH THEY ARE TOO SMALL TO HARM THE HATCHLING, HE STAYS HIDDEN IN THE SHADOWS.

...AND VANISHES INTO THE WOODS. IT IS NOW EARLY EVENING AND THE HATCHLING IS STILL HUNGRY. HE SEES A FALLEN TREE.

HE BEGINS TO EAT THE BARK. THE ROTTING WOOD IS FILLED WITH **NUTRIENTS** THAT THE YOUNG DINOSAUR NEEDS TO GROW.

13

SUDDENLY...

KERACKK!!!

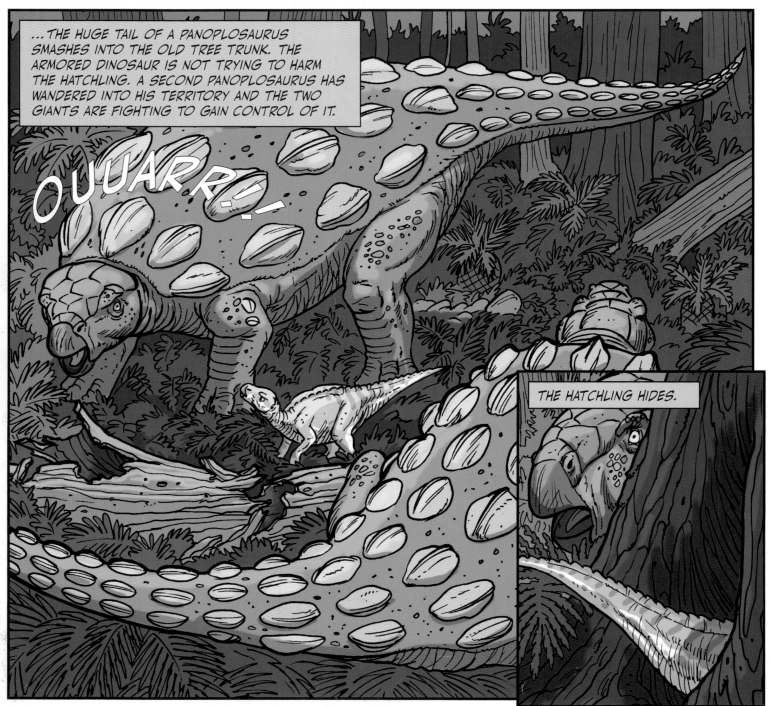

...THE HUGE TAIL OF A PANOPLOSAURUS SMASHES INTO THE OLD TREE TRUNK. THE ARMORED DINOSAUR IS NOT TRYING TO HARM THE HATCHLING. A SECOND PANOPLOSAURUS HAS WANDERED INTO HIS TERRITORY AND THE TWO GIANTS ARE FIGHTING TO GAIN CONTROL OF IT.

OUUARR!!

THE HATCHLING HIDES.

FINALLY, THE FIRST PANOPLOSAURUS CHASES THE OTHER OFF.

IT IS NEARLY DARK WHEN THE PALE HADROSAURUS CREEPS FROM HIS HIDING PLACE. HE TRIES TO REMEMBER THE WAY BACK TO THE NEST SITE.

IT IS NOT SAFE FOR THE SMALL HADROSAURUS TO BE AWAY FROM THE ADULTS AT NIGHT. THE HATCHLING CALLS OUT FOR HIS HERD. HIS SHARP HEARING CATCHES THEIR REPLY. HE ALSO HEARS THE SOUND OF RUSTLING LEAVES.

THERE IS SOMETHING ELSE CLOSE BY...

...AND GETTING CLOSER.

A MEAT-EATING TROODON IS HUNTING. HER LARGE EYES HELP HER SEE IN THE DARK.

THE PALE HATCHLING SETS OFF FOR THE NEST SITE AS QUICKLY AS HE CAN.

THE TROODON'S HUNT IS A SUCCESS.

SHE HAD NOT BEEN HUNTING THE LITTLE HADROSAURUS, BUT A YOUNG ORODROMEUS THAT HAD STRAYED FROM ITS BURROW. SHE TAKES HER KILL BACK TO THE NEST TO FEED HER YOUNG.

THE PALE HATCHLING WAS NEVER TOO FAR FROM THE NEST SITE. AFTER A FEW MINUTES, HE IS BACK AMONG THE ADULTS, SAFE ONCE MORE.

PART THREE... THE WATER HOLE

THE PALE HADROSAURUS IS SIX MONTHS OLD NOW AND NEARLY HALF GROWN. THE HERD HAS SPENT THE LAST FOUR MONTHS ON THE MOVE, TRAVELING TO WHERE THE BEST VEGETATION IS GROWING.

IT IS THE END OF THE DRY SEASON AND THE RAINS ARE LATE. THE FIELDS OF FERNS THAT WERE GREEN AND HEALTHY ARE NOW BROWN AND WILTING. THERE IS LITTLE WATER TO DRINK. THE HADROSAURUSES ARE LOOKING FOR THE WATER HOLE THEY USE EVERY YEAR.

AS THE HADROSAURUSES GET CLOSE, THEY HEAR ANGRY CRIES COMING FROM THE WATER HOLE.

A HERD OF CORYTHOSAURUSES WANT TO DRINK FROM THE WATER HOLE, BUT A GROUP OF ACHELOUSAURUSES STAND IN THEIR PATH. THE HORNED DINOSAURS WAVE THEIR NECKS, TRYING TO SCARE THE CORYTHOSAURUSES AWAY.

MMOOUARHH!

THE FURIOUS CORYTHOSAURUSES ROAR BACK. THEIR HOLLOW HEAD CRESTS MAKE THEIR BOOMING YELLS EVEN LOUDER.

THE HADROSAURUSES ARRIVE.

THE ACHELOUSAURUSES MOVE OFF WHEN THEY SEE THE WHOLE HERD OF HADROSAURUSES.

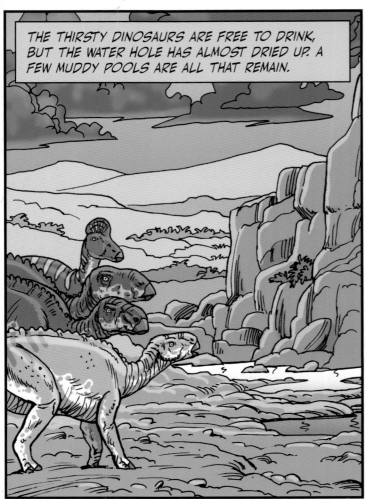

THE THIRSTY DINOSAURS ARE FREE TO DRINK, BUT THE WATER HOLE HAS ALMOST DRIED UP. A FEW MUDDY POOLS ARE ALL THAT REMAIN.

THE PALE HADROSAURUS BENDS DOWN TO DRINK FROM A SLIMY PUDDLE.

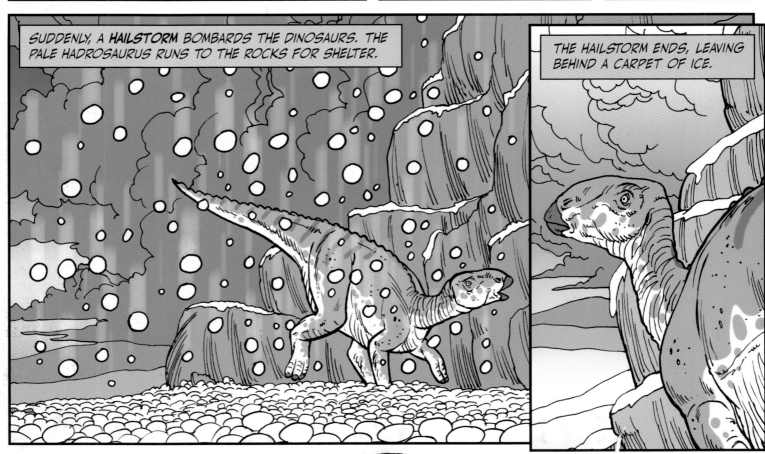

SUDDENLY, A **HAILSTORM** BOMBARDS THE DINOSAURS. THE PALE HADROSAURUS RUNS TO THE ROCKS FOR SHELTER.

THE HAILSTORM ENDS, LEAVING BEHIND A CARPET OF ICE.

WHILE THE GROUND GLEAMS WHITE WITH HAILSTONES, THE CLOUDS HAVE BECOME AS BLACK AS COAL.

THE HAILSTORM WAS JUST THE BEGINNING. A FUNNEL SHAPE STARTS TO GROW FROM THE BOTTOM OF THE CLOUD. IT GETS BIGGER AND BIGGER UNTIL...

...THE FUNNEL OF CLOUD REACHES THE GROUND, KICKING UP A WHIRLING MASS OF DUST AND DIRT. A *TORNADO* HAS FORMED.

THE TORNADO TWISTS RAPIDLY TOWARD THE DINOSAURS. THE TERRIFIED ANIMALS RUN.

THE HERD JOINS THE PALE HADROSAURUS BY THE SHELTERING ROCKS. THE ROAR OF THE TORNADO BECOMES LOUDER AND LOUDER AS IT GETS CLOSER.

RRROOAARHHH!!!

THE TORNADO TEARS THROUGH
THE WATER HOLE. IT IS POWERFUL
ENOUGH TO SMASH LARGE TREES
AND EVEN TOSS AROUND FULL-
GROWN DINOSAURS.

LATER, THE HADROSAURUSES CREEP OUT FROM THE SAFETY OF THE ROCKS.
THE TORNADO HAS GONE, LEAVING THE WATER HOLE LITTERED WITH SMASHED
TREES AND PLANTS. NOT EVERY DINOSAUR HAS ESCAPED SAFELY. A
CORYTHOSAURUS LIES DEAD. THERE IS NO SIGN OF THE ACHELOUSAURUSES.

AS THE DINOSAURS GAZE
AT THE STORM DAMAGE, IT
BEGINS TO RAIN. THE WET
SEASON HAS STARTED.
THERE WILL BE ENOUGH
WATER FOR EVERY ANIMAL,
AND THE FERN FIELDS WILL
BECOME GREEN AGAIN.

PART FOUR

HOME AGAIN

IT HAS BEEN 10 MONTHS SINCE THE HERD LEFT THE NEST SITE. THEY HAVE TRAVELED IN A BIG CIRCLE AND ARE NEARLY BACK WHERE THEY BEGAN.

THEY HAVE FINALLY REACHED THE RIVER ESTUARY.

THE HERD LEADER IS NERVOUS, THOUGH. HE SENSES THAT SOMETHING IS NOT RIGHT.

SUDDENLY, A GROUP OF ORNITHOMIMUSES BURSTS OUT OF THE FOREST.

THEY ARE FOLLOWED BY A MEAT-EATING DRYPTOSAURUS.

THE HADROSAURUSES PANIC. LIFTING THEMSELVES UP ONTO THEIR BACK LEGS, THEY GALLOP AFTER THE ORNITHOMIMUSES. THE DRYPTOSAURUS IS NOT BIG ENOUGH TO HURT AN ADULT, BUT IT COULD KILL A YOUNG HADROSAURUS.

THE DRYPTOSAURUS SEES THE PALE HADROSAURUS...

...AND CHASES AFTER HIM. THE HADROSAURUS SPLASHES INTO THE RIVER TO ESCAPE, BUT THE DRYPTOSAURUS FOLLOWS.

BROOSH!!

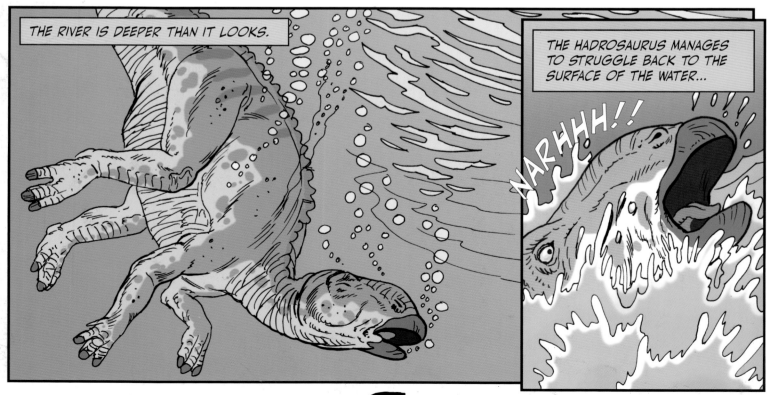

THE RIVER IS DEEPER THAN IT LOOKS.

THE HADROSAURUS MANAGES TO STRUGGLE BACK TO THE SURFACE OF THE WATER...

NARHHH!!

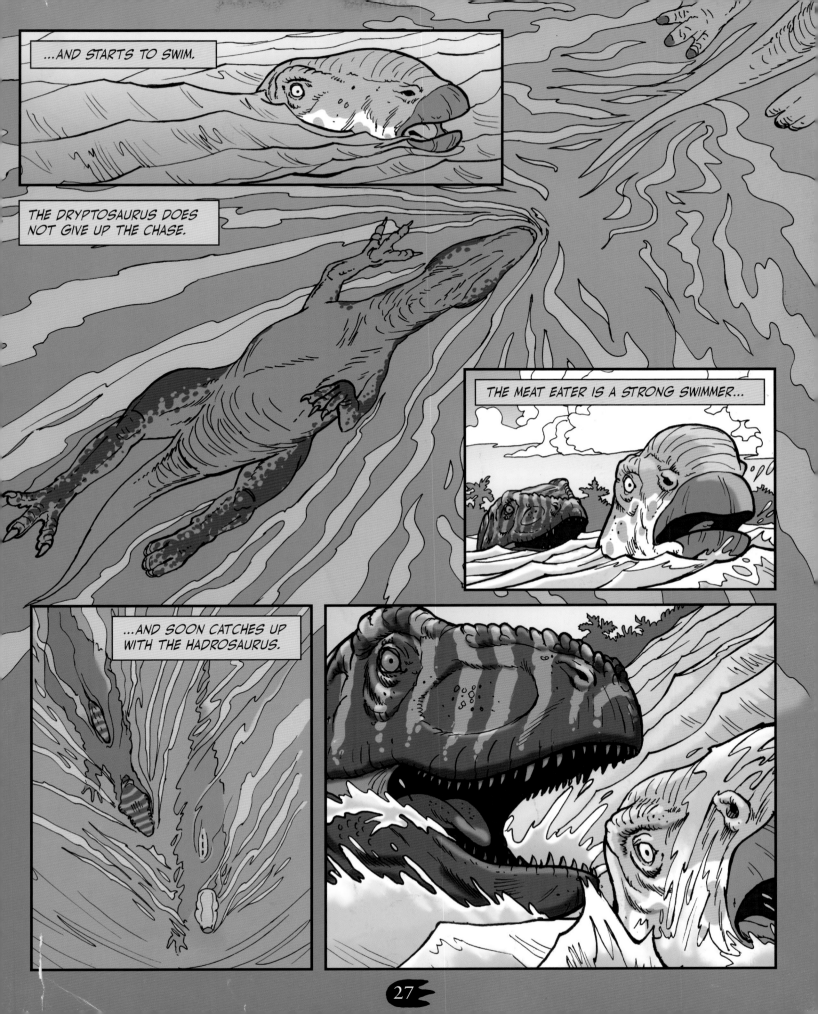

...AND STARTS TO SWIM.

THE DRYPTOSAURUS DOES NOT GIVE UP THE CHASE.

THE MEAT EATER IS A STRONG SWIMMER...

...AND SOON CATCHES UP WITH THE HADROSAURUS.

ALONG WITH THE HADROSAURUSES, THE DEINOSUCHUS HAS ALSO RETURNED TO THE ESTUARY. IT ATTACKS THE DRYPTOSAURUS, LIFTING IT OUT OF THE WATER.

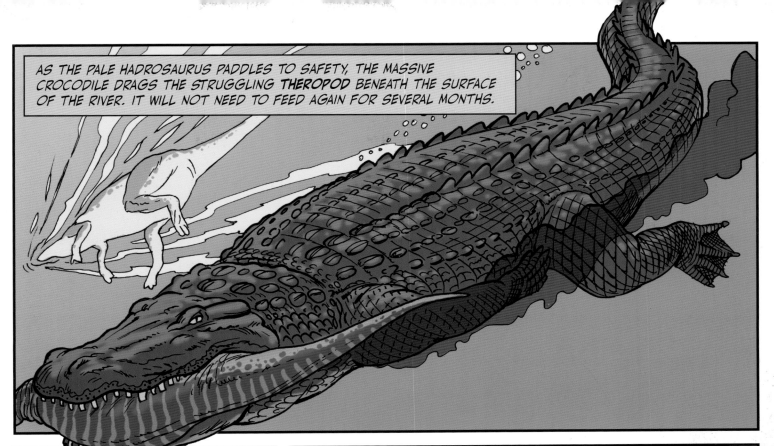

AS THE PALE HADROSAURUS PADDLES TO SAFETY, THE MASSIVE CROCODILE DRAGS THE STRUGGLING **THEROPOD** BENEATH THE SURFACE OF THE RIVER. IT WILL NOT NEED TO FEED AGAIN FOR SEVERAL MONTHS.

HE SWIMS TO THE RIVERBANK, CLIMBS BACK ONTO DRY LAND...

...AND REJOINS THE HERD. IN A FEW HOURS, THEY WILL BE AT THE NEST SITE, WHERE NEW NESTS WILL BE BUILT AND EGGS LAID. IN THE MEANTIME, HE WILL KEEP CLOSE TO THE HERD AND LEARN HOW TO STAY ALIVE.

FOSSIL EVIDENCE

SCIENTISTS LEARN WHAT DINOSAURS MAY HAVE LOOKED LIKE BY STUDYING THEIR FOSSIL REMAINS. FOSSILS ARE FORMED WHEN THE HARD PARTS OF AN ANIMAL OR PLANT ARE BURIED AND TURN TO ROCK OVER THOUSANDS OF YEARS.

In 1858, a nearly complete fossilized dinosaur skeleton was found by a fossil hunter named William Foulke at Haddonfield, New Jersey. It was called Hadrosaurus, and the mounted dinosaur (bottom) went on view for the public 10 years later. Before then, scientists thought that dinosaurs were like very large lizards that walked with their stomachs held just above the ground. The mounted skeleton showed the Hadrosaurus standing on its back legs, as tall as a house.

For the first time, people had a good idea of what dinosaurs looked like. Today the fossil is shown in a more accurate pose (below). Recently, fossils belonging to close relatives of Hadrosaurus have been found. These show what its skin looked like (inset), how big its muscles were, and even what its heart, lungs, and other organs looked like.

ANIMAL GALLERY

Bambiraptor
"Baby raider"
Length: 2.5 ft (75 cm)
A small, meat-eating dinosaur that probably had feathers.

Orodromeus
"Mountain runner"
Length: 6 ft (2 m)
A small, plant-eating dinosaur that may have lived in burrows.

Troodon
"Wounding tooth"
Length: 6.5 ft (2 m)
A meat-eating dinosaur that was highly intelligent.

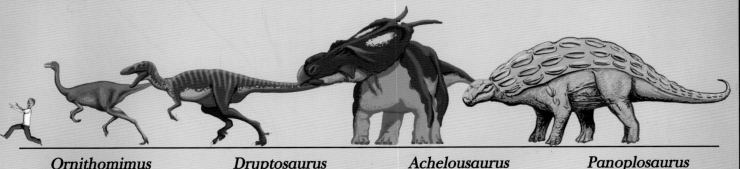

Ornithomimus
"Bird mimic"
Length: 12 ft (4 m)
A fast-running dinosaur that ate insects, reptiles, mammals, and plants.

Dryptosaurus
"Tearing lizard"
Length: 20 ft (6 m)
A medium-sized meat eater that had 8-inch (20 cm) claws on its fingers.

Achelousaurus
"Achelous's lizard"
Length: 20 ft (6 m)
A plant eater whose skull was over 5 feet (1.5 m) long.

Panoplosaurus
"Fully armored lizard"
Length: 23 ft (7 m)
The plant-eating Panoplosaurus was covered with bony plates that protected it from its enemies.

Deinosuchus
"Terrible crocodile"
Length: 40 ft (12 m)
A huge crocodile with a bite twice as strong as any present-day animal.

Quetzalcoatlus
"Bird serpent"
Wingspan: 33 ft (10 m)
A reptile and one of the world's largest flying animals.

Corythosaurus
"Helmet lizard"
Length: 35 ft (10.5 m)
A large, plant-eating dinosaur that may have used its crest to make loud, low-pitched calls.

GLOSSARY

carrion (KAR-ee-un) Dead animals.

Cretaceous period (krih-TAY-shus PIR-ee-ud) The time between 145 million and 65 million years ago.

estuary (ES-choo-wer-ee) An area of water where the ocean meets a river.

fossils (FO-sulz) The remains of living things that have turned to rock.

graze (GRAYZ) To feed on grass or other plants.

hailstorm (HAYL-storm) A storm that drops small pieces of ice.

nutrients (NOO-tree-unts) Foods that help living things grow.

theropod (THIR-uh-pod) The group of dinosaurs that are meat eaters.

tornado (tor-NAY-doh) A funnel-shaped cloud formed from powerful winds.

INDEX

Web Sites

Due to the changing nature of Internet links, the Rosen Publishing Group, Inc., has developed an online list of Web sites related to the subject of this book. This site is updated regularly. Please use this link to access the list:

www.powerkidslinks.com/gdino/hadro/